# SEEING JESUS
*Through*
# MY EYES

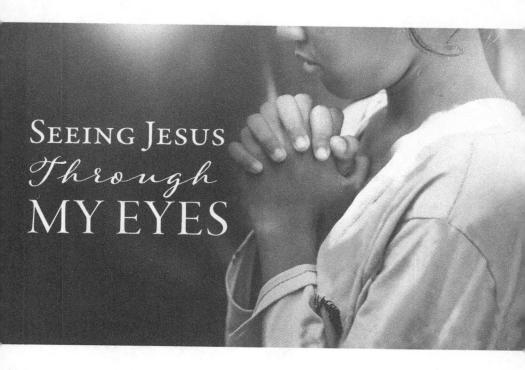

# Seeing Jesus Through MY EYES

## Loretta Jones-Tensley

XULON PRESS

Xulon Press
2301 Lucien Way #415
Maitland, FL 32751
407.339.4217
www.xulonpress.com

Unless otherwise indicated, Scripture quotations taken from the King James
Version (KJV) – *public domain*.

Paperback ISBN-13: 978-1-66281-567-6
Ebook ISBN-13: 978-1-66281-568-3

# TABLE OF CONTENTS

# PREFACE

Thank you and welcome to all who have chosen to share with me this great experience; From my heart and soul to the minds and spirits of all who read this book.

I honor Jesus Christ as head of my life, and praise Him for the gift He gave me in expressing myself through writing.

I enjoy sharing the positivity and testimonies of the goodness and mercies of Christ. Life can sometimes have you feeling like you are the only one on a vicious roller coaster ride. This is my attempt to reach as many souls as possible and share the news of the Savior of this world, Jesus Christ, to let YOU know you are not alone.

I have been writing poetry since the age of twelve. Though I can recall pads and tablets being misplaced or lost, I do still have several writings of over forty-some odd years.

Although there is nothing specific that puts me in the mode to write, the journey of life itself, with all its twists and turns, ups and downs, highs and lows, events and lack thereof, always puts something in mind to express.

Recognizing my parents, Frank and Annie Jones, for all the lessons taught and learned, and many thanks for helping me get started on this chapter in my life, my book. I am also grateful to my children, my F.R.E.D. (Francheska, Rayanna, Emmanuel, Destiny) for this great computer they gifted me to get started publishing.

In all the years I have been writing, I have only published one piece. It has been my habit to write and then store away what I had written, with the dream of one day publishing it all.

In 2004, my half-sister, Adena Hill, lost her mother Reva. Over time, we became, and are still, very close. I put myself in her shoes and... the rest is history. The poem I wrote was inspired with her in mind, and I titled it, "But I know." It was published in 2006.

So, thank you to Xulon Press for this amazing opportunity. My hope and prayer is that within the bindings/covers of this book, you find hope, inspiration, joy, peace, and love to keep "fighting the good fight."

Praying that as you read these pages, you will let them be absorbed in your spirit; that they can then be shared with someone else and so on and so on; hence, spreading the goodness of a life in Christ.

Many thanks to you all and God bless.

# HEAVEN

A year is a long time
To look back and evaluate
One day at a time; up to now,
Tallying the progress you've made.

Did you meet all the goals you set,
Or most of them, anyway?
If tonight was your last night on earth,
Is six feet under where your soul would stay?

Would you rise like the phoenix?
Your earthly deeds completed
Done well enough for the Master's approval.
Relieved, you haven't been deleted.

In that great Book of Life,
Your name bares a check, instead of an X.
You weren't x-ed out at all.
Your name He called next.

That satisfied, exuberant feeling,
Realizing your work wasn't in vain.
Your mistakes you made, you corrected; He forgave.
And now He has called your name.

No more stress, no more heartaches.
No mistreatment and being left out.
The work you did to make it here
Was all worthwhile, no doubt.

No one here to dismantle,
To judge what's not good enough.
The insufficiencies of this 'ole world
We're all covered by His blood.

Mistakes were all forgiven.
Deliberate acts washed away.
No more wandering around that dressing room called earth.
You're home now, and here you will stay.

# JUDGING

Because I care about
The love that You give to me,
I'll live my life to serve You;
That others watching will see.

The old me, some will recall,
The goodness observed won't be
The me that used to exist.
Your goodness they won't see.

Blinded by what used to be,
We were all in the same boat.
When I dared to jump out and be different,
They hoped I'd sink rather than float.

Why would I break away,
Come out of my comfort zone;
Searching for something different,
Leaving behind the same 'ole same 'ole ?

Not because I thought
I was better in any way,
But the day after day of the same thing
Had become all too mundane.

Of all the regrets this life has held,
Following You I wish I'd done sooner.
How great it is to be on Your path;
So bright now is my future.

# HATS OFF TO YOU, LORD

All the things You said You'd do, I know Your Word didn't lie. And all those times I slipped back, and You could have just passed me by.

For the times I knew I was doing wrong, but did it anyway, Jesus, You know I'm thankful, to You and the Father today.

When I'd watch TV and not read the Word, or party when I should have been in church, you kept Your hand right over me, Lord; You loved me just that much.

When I'd swear and curse and do even worst, Lord, You were still right there. Though I neglected to thank You, the rod on me You did spare.

When I was sassy to my mom and, at a time, hated my dad, Lord, You know I thank You for the compassion You did have.

So my hat's off to You, Lord, for taking my mind out of a whirl, cause You said, "Greater is He that is in me, than he that is in the world (1 John 4:4)."

# MATTHEW 26: 39
# DIVINELY ALIGNED

When I can't think of nothing  to say,
And my mind is all but blank,
Jesus, Jesus, Jesus!
To Him, I give all my thanks.

Protection from dangers, seen and unseen,
Blessings I don't deserve
Provisions all handed to me,
More than what I'm worth.

How much DO I owe Him?
Really, how much do I owe?
He didn't give up when rejected.
All thirty-three years He did go.

Man's rejections, His own not owning Him;
And yet, He kept right on
In spite of all we did to Him.
He still made it to His throne.

Divinely aligned, just for my good,
Knowing I would mess up.
FOR ME, He asked His Father
About removing THAT CUP.

Oh, I'm so glad He drank it,
Every sip, through the bitter end.
And now I know where I'm headed.
In hell, my life won't end.

It's all so much to fathom,
So, "Thank you," is what I say.
So relieved He accepts it and counts it to my good,
And allows me to be on my way.

The same 'ole prayers, said every night;
A different one He doesn't demand.
The same blessings and new ones added
They're all in His plan.

"Thank you, thank you, thank you"
Is my repetitive prayer every day.
To number my thanks, with each rising sun;
How many I cannot say.

# JESUS CAN WORK IT OUT

"Love and happiness," Al Green sings.
That's what sums up life.
Something so strong, it'll make you do wrong;
Yet overwhelm you to do right.

That thing that hurts you so bad,
Human instinct wants to make it stop;
Yet a spirit within wars against.
There is no need for you to plot.

Rest assured, there is a way
To calm the spirits within.
Invite in your heart Jesus Christ.
That's the sure way to win.

# FOR THE THINGS YOU HAVE DONE

I'll forever praise You, Lord; let nothing get in my way. For You've proven Yourself to me, Lord, upon this very day.

I'll let nothing turn me around – best friend, boyfriend, or loved ones. I'll keep my trust in You at all times, to ensure myself of our oneness.

Jesus, You know I thank you, and oh so very much – for giving me just one more chance before You gave me up.

I will ever praise You, Lord; all the honor and glory is Yours – because without You, a long time ago, on my life You could have closed the doors.

# GRATEFULNESS

Thank you God, for allowing me
To lay it all on You.
You never throw it back in my face
With the challenge of "what now to do."

Issue after issue
I've left laying at your feet.
No matter the case or enormity,
You've worked it out for me.

By Your stripes, I am healed.
My sins, forgotten in THAT sea.
So many promises You said You'd uphold
All laid out for me.

Diligently, I do my best,
Painstaking at times it is;
But following Your map for this journey,
One day, with You, I will live.

# IN GOD

Oh, that the world would see.
To have it all, it's God we need.
Health and riches, peace of mind;
In Him only, them all we find.

Oh, that the world would see.
To have it all, it's God we need.
The struggles that may go straight up hill,
Trusting in Him, they would have to yield.

Oh, that the world would see.
To have it all, it's God we need.
No one would be, better than the other.
We'd love each other, as sisters and brothers.

Oh, that the world would see.
To have it all, it's God we need.
Not color nor status to separate;
No barriers at all to break.
Equal, and the same we'd be,
To have it all, it's God we need.

# FOLLOW HIS LEAD

With Jesus leading,
You can't go wrong.
With Him ahead,
You're sure to make it "home."

If you let Jesus lead you,
Allow Him to take the helm,
You'll never be stranded or have to abandon.
Your ship will always sail.

If you let Jesus lead you,
Allow Him to direct your path,
Wrong turns, there will never be;
No suffering from aftermaths.

If you let Jesus lead you,
From morning through your day to night,
Your cares of this world will be minimal.
All of them, He will make alright.

# COUNTING MY BLESSINGS – AGAIN

Today, I'm counting my blessings, as I oftentimes do.
How I wish, long, and pray for things I want from You.

I reflect on things in my life that aren't so savory, but still.
You answer and meet my needs, even desires You fulfill.

I thought of earlier today, if I had ten thousand tongues,
How easy it would be to praise You with at least some.

YOU constructed this vessel that doesn't require as many;
But the single one You've provided, I can praise You with it a plenty.

Things, money, requests: each one I make known.
Needing, requiring, remembering the many seeds I have sewn.

Yet, in my distress, I can still depend on You
Forever and ever, amen. I know You will always bring me through.

# CORONAVIRUS CHAOS

"No weapon formed against me shall prosper"
Says Isaiah 54 (:17)
My faith, my belief, my hope in You
Assures me of that and more.

When all the world is in chaos,
Confusion all around,
I just look to You Lord,
And my mind escapes the sound.

Stand for something or fall for anything,
It's been said, time and again.
So I stand with the One who has everything
And eternity in His hands.

No weapon formed against me shall prosper
This, I do truly believe.
In His will, on His path I'll live,
And He will take care of me.

So I will always praise You
In all that I go through.
I will always praise You
Cause that's how I make it through.

# I WANNA BE IN THE NUMBER

I want to make it to heaven and see my Jesus' face. To hear Him say, "Well done servant," on that great and holy day.

I'm striving every day, to be perfect just like Him. I'm watching all I do and say, to be sure I make it in.

I want to see you all there, not to hear Christ tell you good-bye. I want you to be there forever, to live in that sweet by-and-by.

Can you imagine what a day that will be, shouting and rejoicing in Him? Thanking Jesus, praising His holy name, because He'd brought you in.

In from a world of sin and disgrace, never more to enter in. The sinner will be asking for water or some shade; but me, I'll just be praising my Savior's name.

What about you? What will you be doing?

# HIS LOVE

Talking about Your goodness
And the care You give to me.
Sharing the wealth of gifts in my soul
And how You allow me to be.

Happy and blessed beyond my deserving,
Giving You all the praise,
Expressing and loving this "new me,"
I'm basking in Your grace.

When I look on the year before
And the year before, the year before that,
Webster has not yet the definitions
Of all there is to grasp.

Happiness in living, however I choose,
But choosing to live pleasing You.
Counting my blessings with each passing day,
Starting every morning anew.

# IT'S PERSONAL

YOU gave all You had,
In case I chose to do right.
Counting my blessings is what I do:
Morning, noon, and night.

Knowing I'd mess up, over and over,
You still chose to give Your life.
You could have said, "Lord, just a trial period,"
But You took Your Father to be serious.

You said, "If she doesn't praise me,
I'll cause the rocks to cry out."
YOU can use anything because You are God.
How dare I give way for something else to shout?

Over and over and over again,
Your Word proves who You are.
Why mess with perfection? Why try on my own,
When You've covered it all by far?

# HAPPINESS IS...

Happiness is feeling, so good inside
That you can't stop the joy from flowing, from your lips or from your eyes.

Happiness is knowing, sooner or later you'll get an answer.
It may not be as soon as you think, but it won't be too late either.

Happiness is knowing, you've got a God that's always there.
Nobody has to keep Him posted, because He's always aware.

He sees you in your troubled times, and He sees you when you're alright.
He sees you joyful all day long, and when you moan and weep at night.

So He sends something, down from above, just to let you know,
Without this finger of love He spares, you and I would be no moe'.

# ALL RED

The blood that Jesus shed for you,
Or was it shed for me?
I dare not speak for others,
Cause we might disagree.

Because my status in living
Is in a class, yours is not.
Does that blood disregard me?
Am I in a different pot?

The blood that Jesus shed for you,
Or was it shed for me?
I dare not speak for others,
Cause we might disagree.

My appearance does not show
The same hue as is yours.
Your house is larger than mine.
But to enter, we both need doors.

The blood that Jesus shed for you,
Or was it shed for me?
I dare not speak for others,
Cause we might disagree.

Your bank account is always full,
For nothing do you lack.
My balance teeters moderately,
With some but not much slack.

The blood that Jesus shed for you,
Or was it shed for me?
I dare not speak for others,
Cause we might disagree.

The blood that Jesus shed
Was shed to cover all.
John 3:16 says, "WHOSOEVER"
So that includes us ALL.

# LIVING TESTIMONY

I only call on Jesus,
Cause He's the only one.
No one's son or daughter died for me.
God gave His only Son.

I only call on Jesus.
My best friend doesn't always have the answer.
I didn't feel a thing; I thought I was okay.
But the doctor said it was cancer.

I only called on Jesus,
As the car headed toward the ditch.
Like an eagle soaring in open sky,
I came through it without a stitch.

I've only called on Jesus
For this and that and the other,
Cause I knew of nothing or no one at all
To take care of it all – no – not even my mother.

# LET JESUS FIX IT FOR YOU

God is a good God.
He can only be.
God is a good God,
Cause look what He's done for me.

When I was sinking deep in sin,
He didn't just let me drown.
He looked upon me then.
He sent some help on down.

The Father came, stretched out His hand,
And said, "Come unto me, daughter"
He said, "Let me help you out of this
Before you go any farther."

So I grabbed His hand, got a strong grip,
And closed my eyes real tight.
Then with one pull He saved me,
And from then on I was alright.

Whenever I got in a situation
That I knew I just couldn't handle,
I looked up and said, "Lord, won't You help me,
Before this becomes a scandal?"

And do you know what – God heard me,
And He answered me right away.
He said, "Hold on, daughter; I'm coming to your rescue.
Cause I don't want you to suffer this way."

He handled the problem in such a way
He didn't even lose His cool.
That enemy He saved me from then
Today is now my footstool.

# LIMBO

With desperate times come desperate measures;
It's what the devil wants you to concede.
But faith and hope and trust in God
Is what you really need.

Weights and measures, what if's and what might's.
Headaches all day long
To choose one and forget the other.
Somewhere you just might go wrong.

Give it to Jesus, all of your problems,
Cause really He IS the only one.
Without guessing or assuming, wishing or wanting:
With Him, peace and happiness will come.

He's not always there when you want Him to be,
But never ever is He late.
And when all is said and done,
We are ever so grateful for the wait.

# ST. JOHN 14:13

In the name of Jesus,
Only in "that name"
Do I have victory.
The Word says I can ask,
Claim a thing in faith.
And in the name of Jesus, it will be.

# YOU DID IT LORD, AND I THANK YOU

You said You'd make a way, when there seemed to be no way. You said You'd make THE WAY, if I would fast and pray.

When there seemed to be no rainbow, after the storm had gone, You told me Lord, not to search the skies, but deep within my soul.

So I searched my soul – inside and out — but that rainbow I still couldn't find. Then You told me Lord, not to rush it, but to give it a little time.

I gave it one day and then another, three days I stayed before You. And upon that fourth day, it happened – and I knew Lord, it could only be You.

You said that prayer changes things, and the hardest comes with time. You said when I got down to my very last, You'd come just in the nick of time.

Nobody but You Lord, nobody but You, I know it was nobody but You. I asked for it and believed – You did it for me Lord, and I thank you.

# YES

Am I too close to the mirror?
I am, yes I think I am.
Calvary afforded me
All I could not see.

Am I too close to the mirror?
I am, I really do believe.
All the dwelling on the reasons
I still cannot see.

Am I too close to the mirror?
I just got to be.
In all I try to figure,
I still don't see what it is You see in me.

So, I'll just continue to thank you,
To worship You and give You praise.
I'll walk in Your will and ways
For the duration of my days.

# VALUE

Thank you, Lord, for never growing weary.
You just don't ever get tired
Of hearing our petitions and needs we pour out,
Trying to do what you require.

Following the "Good Book's" instructing,
Laid out for this journey called life.
Doing our best to abide in Your will,
Because we know it's right.

There are times we may slip,
Might stumble and even fall.
But the multitude of our sins
Your blood covers them all.

Heartaches and headaches
Pressing toward that prize,
Praying our endeavors on this roller coaster.
Be acceptable in Your sight.

So thank you, Lord, for never tiring,
Not ever giving up on me.
For accepting all my efforts,
Your face, I am striving to see.

# UNWORTHY

It's not cause I'm so good
That things are going so well.
I just do my best
To avoid that road to hell.

Though perfect I am not,
Flawed like everyone else,
I choose to depend on God,
Not on myself or wealth.

I try my best to praise You,
While going through the storms,
So when it is all over,
By Your grace, it can do me no harm.

Because You paid it all.
At the cross, the ground is level.
There's room for all in Your kingdom
Black – Red – White – and Yellow.

# LOST – SEARCHING FOR ANSWERS

Draw Your children closer to You:
The ones that choose to ignore;
The ones that do know of You,
But will not open their doors.

The hearts that are broken
And shattered into pieces.
The lies that they've believed
That left them feeling defeated.

The souls that are lost,
Searching in despair.
The cure-all they've depended on
That is no longer there.

The mind they are no longer
In control of.
The feel-good that they look for
From any kind a' love.

The longing of eternity
Seen deep in their eyes.
The mirage in the distance;
Just another disguise.

The "better" they wait for
That seems never to come.

Yet always playing games
That can never be won.

Open their eyes, dear Lord,
With peacefulness in view.
Give them the joy they lack
With the goodness of following You.

# I CAN'T SWIM

JUST like that big ship
Battered and torn by the sea,
Trial after trial and battle after battle,
My God keeps on keeping me.

Whenever the ball lands in my court,
And my next move I haven't fathomed,
Caught off guard but His Holy Spirit
Shows me my next pattern.

There is no greater leader I know of,
Onward and upward, I can't fail.
Maybe battered and maybe torn
But this is one ship that will continue to sail.

# EVEN RUNNIN' ON EMPTY

Sometimes to say, "I bless you, Lord,"
Seems menial to say the least.
Your strength continually lifts me
Every time I am weak.

My prayer, my thoughts, my alms to You
Will never be enough.
But forever I will lift You high,
I'll never, ever give up.

On trying my best to please You
Of longing for Your "okay,"
I'll keep You close – my Savior,
On this journey all the way.

At times when I might lose my way,
Stumble in uncertainty,
I'll say a prayer and shout a praise;
A hymn with authority.

I may retreat to my corner
And shed a few tears,
But I'll hang on to that still, soft voice,
Repeating in my ears

Like that small engine
That kept repeating, "I think I can."
I'll keep pressing toward Your kingdom.
For YOU, I'm taking that stand.

I'll keep hiding behind that mountain,
Shielded from the rough, cold winds.
I won't give up; I just can't.
Cause with You I know I'll win.

How can I forget
All the times You've rescued me?
What I care about – You care even more.
Over and over, You let me see.

All of those "close calls"
When death was right there.
You spared me and comforted me.
You showed how much You cared.

So yeah, sometimes I get a bit crazy
At the awesomeness of Your love.
I'll keep working in Your vineyard
On my way to meet You above.

# THE WEIGHT

Must Jesus bare the cross alone,
And you and you go free?
I beg to differ, I'll carry mine.
With help from Him, I'll plead.

This journey is not easy.
I slip, I fall often times.
But God's grace and mercy
Picks me up each time.

Straight up hill, yet teetering,
Balancing the best I can.
Almost to give out,
This cross won't let me stand.

Must Jesus bare my cross also?
On Calvary, He gave
His life to give me mine
That price He chose to pay.

So I will carry MY cross
And balance as best I can,
Slipping and teetering I'll look to Him,
Doing my best to follow His plan.

# THE CHURCH

Everyone cannot be
The leader of a flock.
God appoints that position.
The title for us is not.

The teacher can head the class.
The man, the house and spouse.
But HE alone assigns the leader
To guide and instruct HIS house.

# MERCY

If God required of us,
In full or in part,
The likenesses He distributes,
Where would that leave
The condition of our hearts?

Resenting and/or questioning
The price He chose to pay,
Or grateful and admonishing,
Striving every day.

If God required of us,
In full or in part,
The likenesses He distributes,
Where would that leave
The condition of our hearts?

Doing just enough
To sustain the breath He gives;
Alive with little efforts
Doing just enough to live.

If God required of us,
In full or in part,
The likenesses He distributes,
Where would that leave
The condition of our hearts?

Doing the very best,
With every move and breath we take,
No matter what obstacles come
Would the best of it we would try to make?

If God required of us,
In full or in part,
The likenesses He distributes,
Where would that leave
The condition of our hearts?

Would we take a second look
And try to please the Master
With our lives and our choices,
Or not try and become disasters?

If God required of us,
In full or in part,
The likenesses He distributes,
Where would that leave
The condition of our hearts?

He had a choice to make,
For Himself or for us all.
He could have saved Himself,
Leaving each of us to fall.

Since God requires of us
To show our love of Him,
To ourselves, and to each other,
No one we should leave out on a limb.

# THE FAMILY OF GOD

Today, I'm counting my blessings,
Over and over again.
I'm trying to see me as You have seen,
But over and over – when?

When did You deem me worthy
Of the happiness I possess?
What did I do with my insignificances
That You make out to be my best?

The mustard seed, the mustard seed;
I don't even need the whole one.
Every day, every month, every year it's happened,
All because of Your son.

My losses, my gains, my tears and my pains:
They've all come at great cost.
The happy times and laughter
Still don't amount to Your loss.

All I can do, day after day, is keep on counting,
Honoring, cherishing, and giving You glory,
As my blessings just keep on mounting.

# MY TESTIMONY

If the God I know and serve
Never does a thing else for me,
There is so much He's done already;
His grace and mercies number into infinity.

If I witness no more miracles,
As long as I should live.
I can still keep counting
The many sins of my past He did forgive.

If every time my knees I bend,
To look to Him above,
Still I could get up with reasons
Of how to me – He shows His love.

In all I want and still pray for,
If none of it was granted,
I'd still keep praising God.
Not at all would I be distracted.

My faith, my hope, my trust in Him
To keep on moving ahead,
My past is my reminder
The reasons why He bled.

When cry and hope and wait
Was all there was for me,
My past was my reminder
That was enough for me to see.

More crying and praying and waiting,
It was ahead of me.
My trust in Him I held onto,
He didn't just let me be.

Over and over the same prayers,
The tears that covered them too.
With each situation
His love brought me through.

So I will never get tired.
No, I just can't stop.
I'll give Him praise for all He's done.
I'll praise Him till I drop.

# MY EVERYTHING

If my "Savior's" name was "Mom"
And "rescue" was my "son";
If "faithful" was the name of my "daughters";
If "provider" was my "husband";
And "dependable" my BFF,
Then that would be a whole lot of fathers.

If "healer" was my "niece,"
And "sustainer" my "sister,"
And my "pastor," my "confidant";
If my "bestie" was never too busy, for my beck and call,
For nothing, maybe – I'd ever want.

But God, You are to me,
And You have always been.
There's no wondering who I should call.
You're all these things to me.
So, I don't doubly say,
"YOU are my all -n- all."

# MY PRAYER

Thank you, my Savior,
For another day You've given me.
Thank you for Your protection all night;
For keeping evil, harm, and danger away.

Take me through this day Lord,
With You in front of me.
Keep me in Your will and way,
Covered in Your grace and mercy.

Keep me safe from dangers, seen and unseen.
As I go on my way,
Keep my trust in You strong
With each passing day.
Amen.

# THE END

Start your day with Jesus.
You'll be happy all day long.
Issue after issue,
With Him, they can't hold on.

That feeling of invincibility,
Security in everything,
Start your day with Jesus
And let your praises ring.

To Him, you give them all,
The honor and glory He's due.
Start your day with Jesus.
He'll always see you through.

Start your day with Jesus;
With Him, you can't go wrong.
Your whole day through will be a breeze,
From start to finish, all day long.

CPSIA information can be obtained
at www.ICGtesting.com
Printed in the USA
LVHW031757170521
687666LV00007B/234

9 781662 815676